1ST GRADE PHONICS
Unit 5
Spelling Short Vowels

TABLE OF CONTENTS

IMPORTANT: Please refer to the Teacher Guide for specific scripts, procedures, and words that are represented by pictures.

Throughout this Unit, learners will scan QR codes. Be careful they scan each code individually.

Copyright © 2025 Bright Thinker, Inc. All rights reserved. Reproduction of all or portions of this work is prohibited without express written permission from Bright Thinker, Inc.

LEARN

- Spelling CVC words
- Spelling words with digraphs
- Reading contractions and compound words

VOCABULARY

contraction   compound word

DAILY PAGE GOALS

Day	Complete	Day	Complete	Day	Complete
1	ii–7	7	35–40	13	65–71
2	8–17	8	41–47	14	72–79
3	18–23	9	48–53	15	80–85
4	24–28	10	54–58	16	86–91
5	29–30	11	59–60	17	92–93
6	31–34	12	61–64	18	94–98

Teacher reads all pages to the learners.

Learn:

- Sort CVC words by vowel sounds.

- Spell and read words from List 1.

WRITING PHONOGRAM REVIEW

Listen to and write the phonograms.
Underline any multi-letter phonograms.

WORKING WITH WORDS

You will start learning how to spell. All of the words in this Unit follow the spelling rule for short vowel sounds.

Spelling Rules

Short Vowel Sounds: Most of the time, a short vowel sound is spelled with one vowel letter.

run dash grin

The words in List 1 are CVC words. They begin and end with one consonant. The middle vowel is short.

 **Write the correct answers.**
Read the CVC words. Sort them by vowel sound.

box	tap	kid	cob	web
red	jug	bag	zit	sun

1) **a** as in _____ _____ _____

2) **e** as in _____ _____ _____

3) **i** as in _____ _____ _____

4) **o** as in _____ _____ _____

5) **u** as in _____ _____ _____

3

Listen!

? Circle the correct answers.

6) syllables | 1   2   3   4

7) sounds | 1   2   3   4

✏️ Write and read.

8) _____

? Choose the correct answer.

9) Which reading rule does this word follow?
   - ○ beginning **s**
   - ○ double **s**
   - ○ 1st sound of **c**

Listen!

 **Circle the correct answers.**

| 10) | syllables | 1 | 2 | 3 | 4 |

| 11) | sounds | 1 | 2 | 3 | 4 |

 **Write and read.**

12) _____

 **Choose the correct answer.**

13) What is the syllable type?
- ○ open
- ○ r-controlled
- ○ closed

Listen!

? Circle the correct answers.

14) | syllables | 1 | 2 | 3 | 4 |

15) | sounds | 1 | 2 | 3 | 4 |

✏️ **Write and read.**

16) _____

? Choose the correct answer.

17) The vowel sound is ____.
   ○ short
   ○ long
   ○ r-controlled

18) The cat **sat** on her lap.

19) I will sleep in my **bed.**

20) Henry **hit** the drum with his hands.

SCORE   CORRECT   RESCORE

Learn:

- Read contractions.

- Spell and read words from List 1.

Vocabulary:

contraction *[kŭn´trăk shŭn]* – two words combined to become one shorter word

✏️ **Listen to and write the phonograms.**
Underline any multi-letter phonograms.

WORKING WITH WORDS

There is a shorter way to say two words. A **contraction** is two words combined to become one shorter word.

The word *not* is used in many contractions. The letter **o** is removed. It is replaced with a punctuation mark called an apostrophe.

let + us ⟶ let's

can + not ⟶ can't

let's go

can't go

))) **Listen and repeat the contractions.**

did not → didn't

had not → hadn't

has not → hasn't

is not → isn't

Circle the correct answers.
Which picture describes the sentence?

1) Stan **didn't** feel well.

2) Riley **hasn't** had lunch yet.

3) The pencil **isn't** on the desk.

Listen!

 **Circle the correct answers.**

| 4) | syllables | 1 | 2 | 3 | 4 |

| 5) | sounds | 1 | 2 | 3 | 4 |

 **Write and read.**

6) _____

 **Choose the correct answer.**

7) How many consonants are in the word?
   ○ 3
   ○ 1
   ○ 2

Listen!

Circle the correct answers.

8)	syllables	1	2	3	4

9)	sounds	1	2	3	4

Write and read.

10) _____

Choose the correct answer.

11) What is the syllable type?
- ○ open
- ○ closed
- ○ VCe

Listen!

 **Circle the correct answers.**

| 12) | syllables | 1 | 2 | 3 | 4 |

| 13) | sounds | 1 | 2 | 3 | 4 |

 **Write and read.**

14) _____

 **Choose the correct answer.**

15) Which reading rule does this word follow?
- ○ 2nd sound of **c**
- ○ 1st sound of **c**
- ○ **o** before **m**, **n**, or **v**

Listen!

 **Circle the correct answers.**

16) | syllables | 1 2 3 4 |

17) | sounds | 1 2 3 4 |

 **Write and read.**

18) _____

 **Choose the correct answer.**

19) The vowel sound is ____.
  - ○ short
  - ○ long
  - ○ r-controlled

Write the correct answers.
Sort the words in ABC order.

man	cup	let

20) _____

21) _____

22) _____

Use the word in your own sentence.

fox

23) _____

ACTIVITY: CVC Nonsense Words

**You can read and spell CVC words.
Now read these nonsense words.**

zub	lak	vop	jik	rud
fep	nog	mip	jeb	kez
dul	pab	wix	huv	cag
zin	jop	lub	puv	rik
yat	meb	jup	koz	vam
lig	zed	tib	fob	vut

Learn:

- Divide and read two-syllable words.

- Spell and read words from List 1.

WRITING PHONOGRAM REVIEW

 **Listen to and write the phonograms.**
Underline any multi-letter phonograms.

WORKING WITH WORDS

Sometimes, a vowel followed by the letter **r** is not r-controlled. It may be part of a closed or open syllable. This can happen when the letter **r** is doubled or followed by another vowel.

v c | c v
s o r | r y

Closed   Open

v | c v
s i | r e n

Open   Closed

Mark, divide, and read the VCCV and VCV words.
Remember, underline the multi-letter phonograms first.

erupt

hero

iris

virus

cherry

berry

carry

borrow

19

Listen!

? **Circle the correct answers.**

1)	syllables	1	2	3	4

2)	sounds	1	2	3	4

✏️ **Write and read.**

3) _____

? **Choose the correct answer.**

4) Which reading rule does this word follow?
- ○ 1st sound of **g**
- ○ 2nd sound of **g**
- ○ 4th sound of **y**

Listen!

 **Circle the correct answers.**

5) | syllables | 1 | 2 | 3 | 4 |

6) | sounds | 1 | 2 | 3 | 4 |

 **Write and read.**

7) _____

 **Choose the correct answer.**

8) What is the syllable type?
   - ○ open
   - ○ vowel team
   - ○ closed

Listen!

❓ Circle the correct answers.

| 9) | syllables | 1 | 2 | 3 | 4 |

| 10) | sounds | 1 | 2 | 3 | 4 |

✏️ Write and read.

11) _____

❓ Choose the correct answer.

12) The vowel sound is ____.
- ○ short
- ○ long
- ○ r-controlled

Write the correct answers.
Complete the sentences.

dig   job   not

13) This week, my _____ is to water the plants.

14) We made a wall so the rabbits will _____ get in the garden.

15) I hope they do not _____ holes under the wall.

PHONOGRAM REVIEW

 Listen to and circle the correct phonograms.

1)    nk   gn   kn

2)    oe   ough   oa

3)    a   ay   e

4)    wor   ir   ur

5)    wh   w   wr

6)   c   sh   s

7)   o   ou   ow

8)   ay   ai   au

9)   w   z   x

10)   ur   ear   or

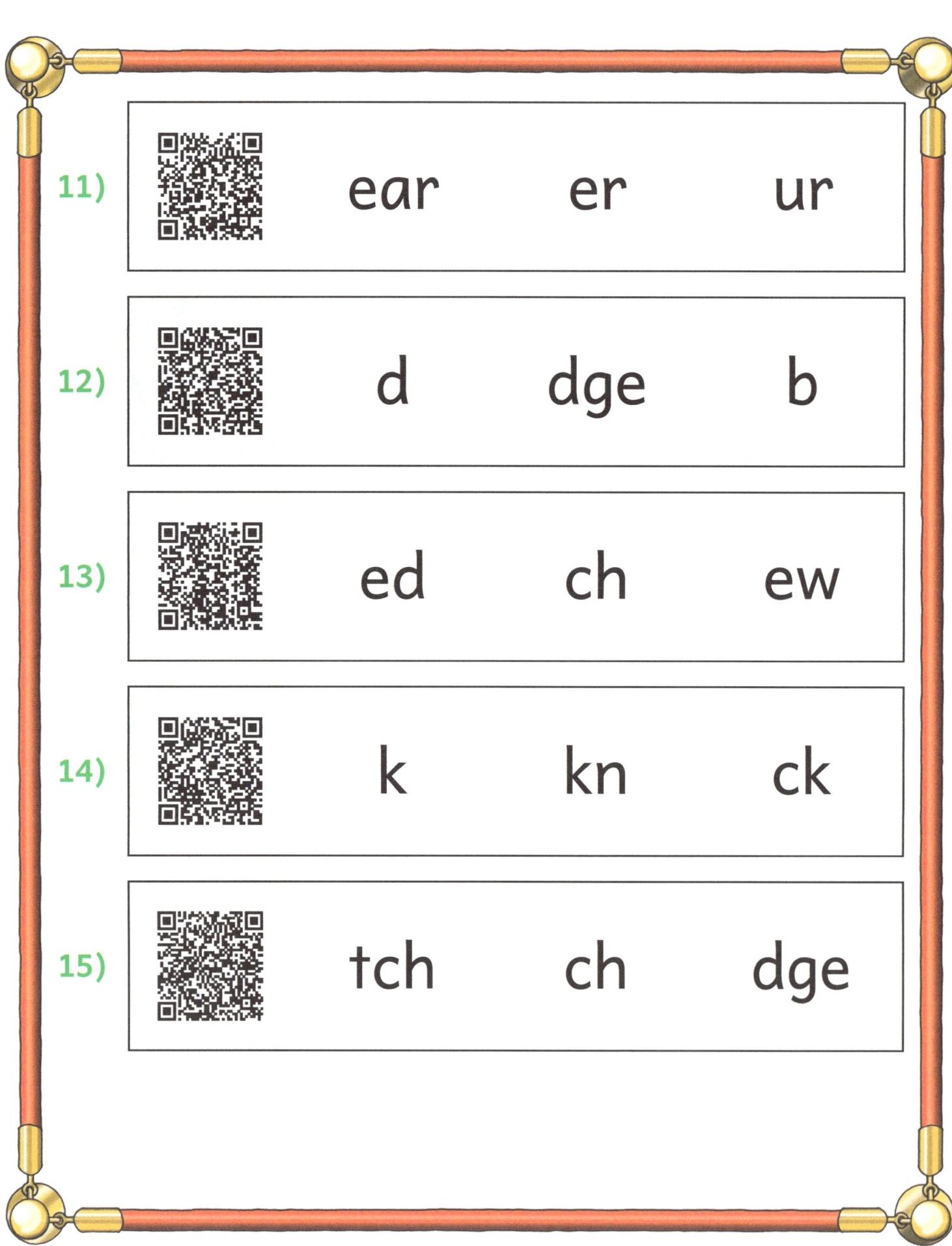

11) ear er ur

12) d dge b

13) ed ch ew

14) k kn ck

15) tch ch dge

26

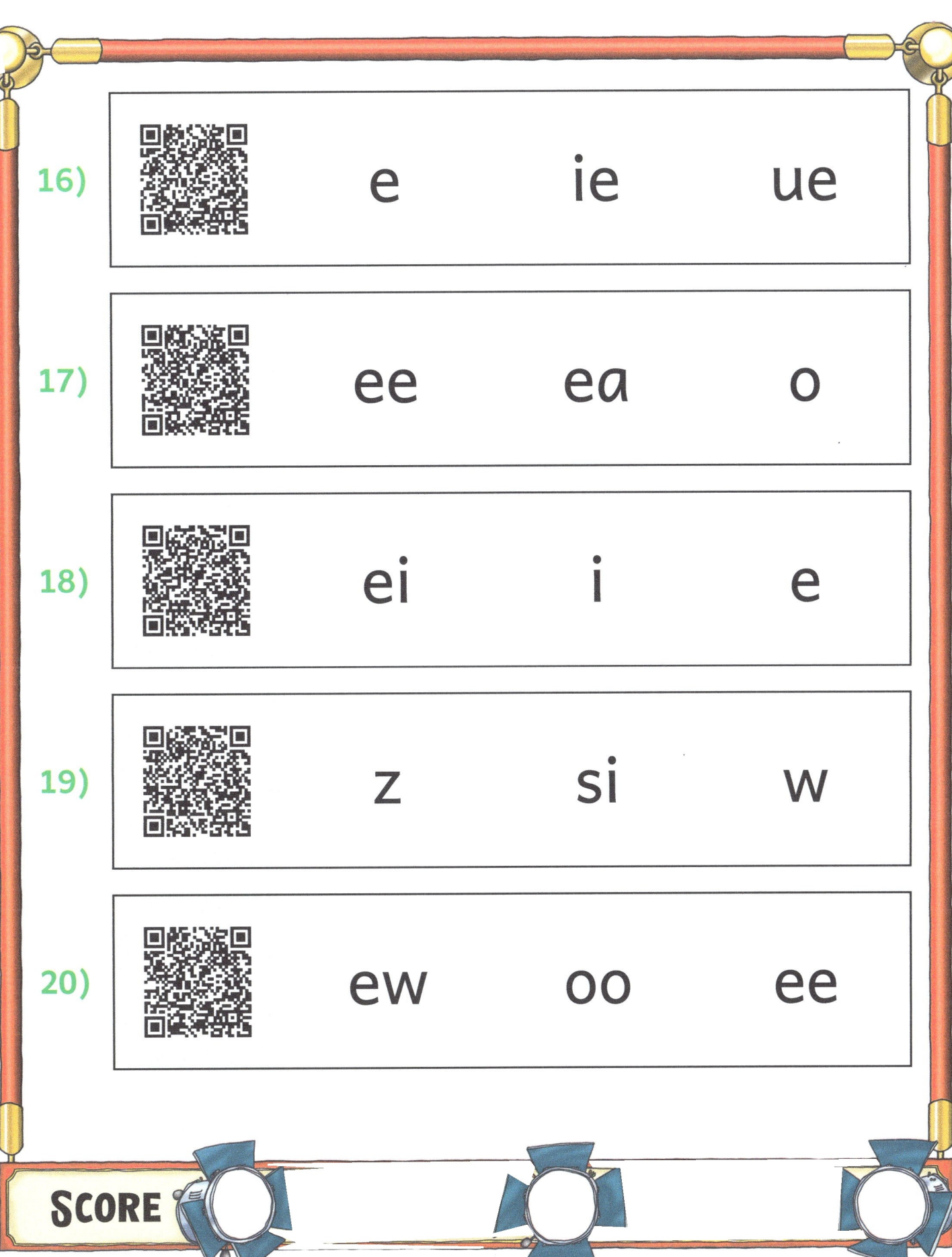

16) e   ie   ue

17) ee   ea   o

18) ei   i   e

19) z   si   w

20) ew   oo   ee

SCORE

SPELLING LIST 1 REVIEW

 **Write the correct answers.**
Sort the words by their vowels.

| fox | sat | man | not | dig |
| let | job | cup | hit | bed |

1) **a** _____ _____

2) **e** _____ _____

3) **i** _____ _____

4) **o** _____ _____ _____

5) **u** _____

READER 8: "Picnic on the Beach"

Reader 8 has the tricky word *of*. It is tricky because the letter **f** makes a **v** sound. It changes the vowel sound. The letter **o** often makes the short **u** sound before the sound of **v**.

Tricky Word
of

 **Write the correct answers.**
Complete the sentences.

sharp   sticky   hot

1) The front of the oven may be _____.

2) The tip of the shovel may be _____.

3) The cover from the honey may be _____.

Reader 8

Picnic on the Beach

 **Choose the correct answers.**

4) Why did the pals go to the beach?
- ○ to go fishing
- ○ to pick up trash
- ○ to have a picnic

5) Why did Quack dig?
- ○ to take a nap
- ○ to make a sand castle
- ○ to get a shell

6) Why did Zip hit a bell?
- ○ to wake up the pals
- ○ to make music
- ○ to tell the time

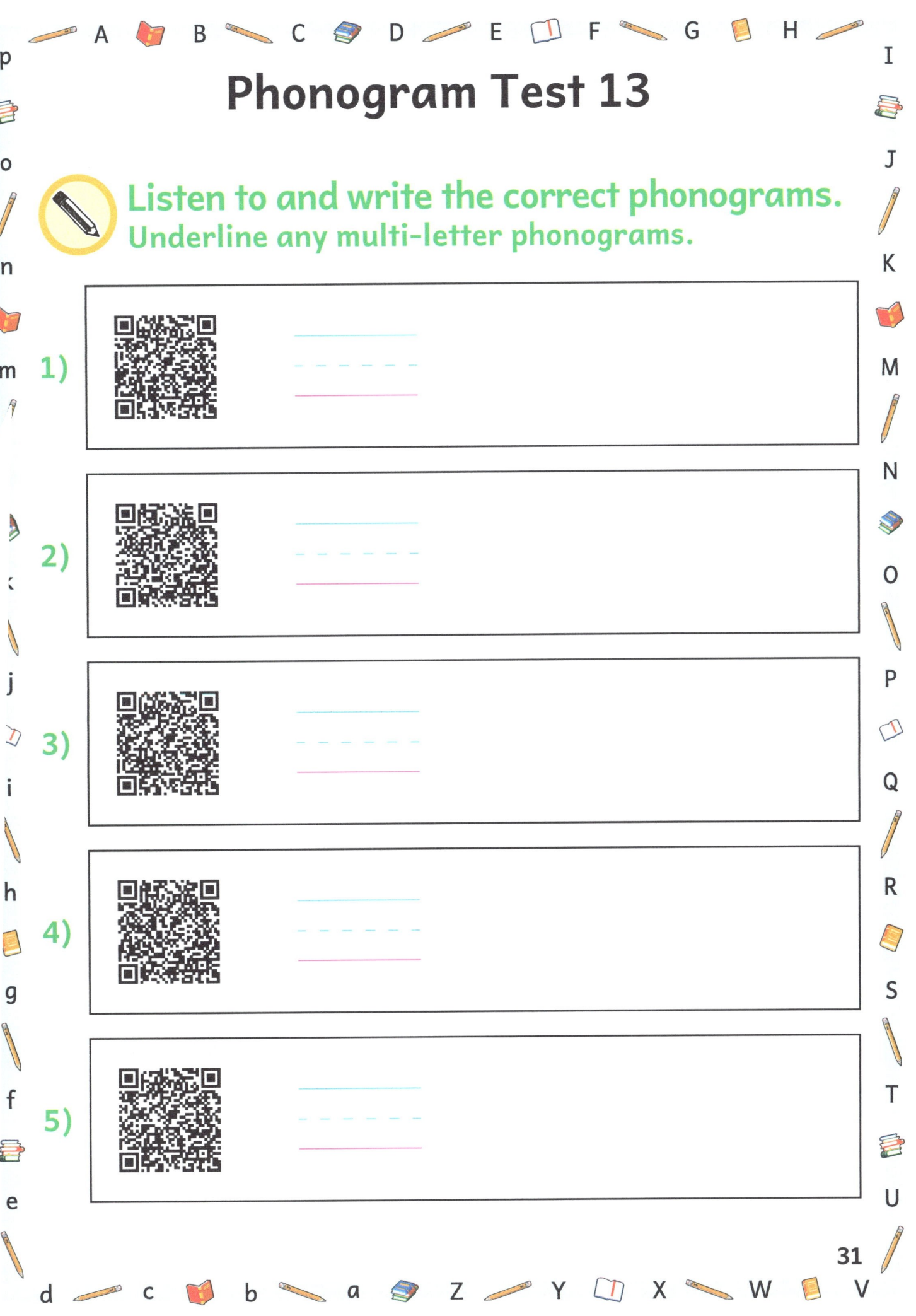

Phonogram Test 13

Listen to and write the correct phonograms.
Underline any multi-letter phonograms.

1)

2)

3)

4)

5)

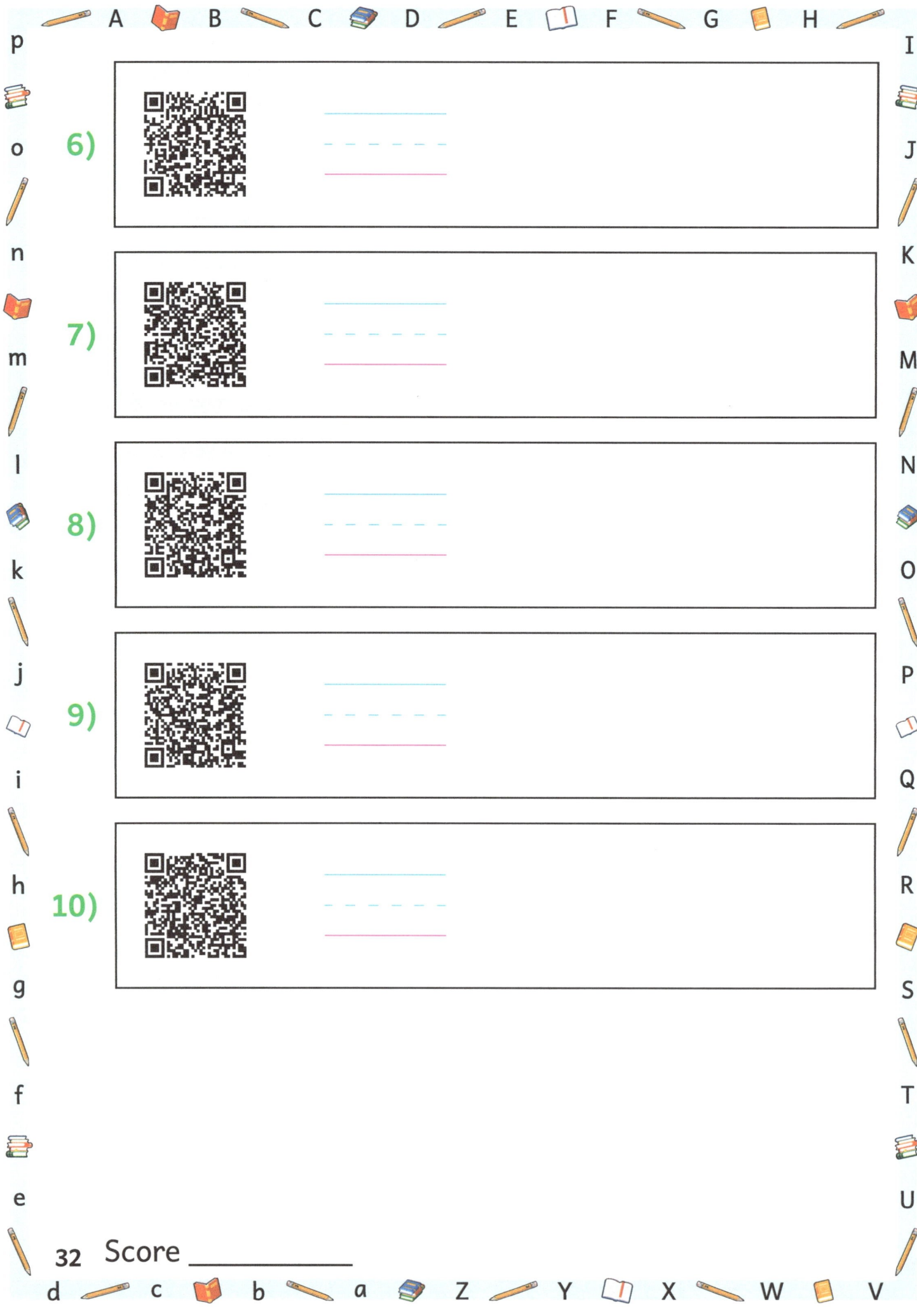

A B C D E F G H I J K M N O P Q R S T U V W X Y Z a b c d e f g h i j k l m n o p

6)

7)

8)

9)

10)

32 Score _____

Spelling Test List 1

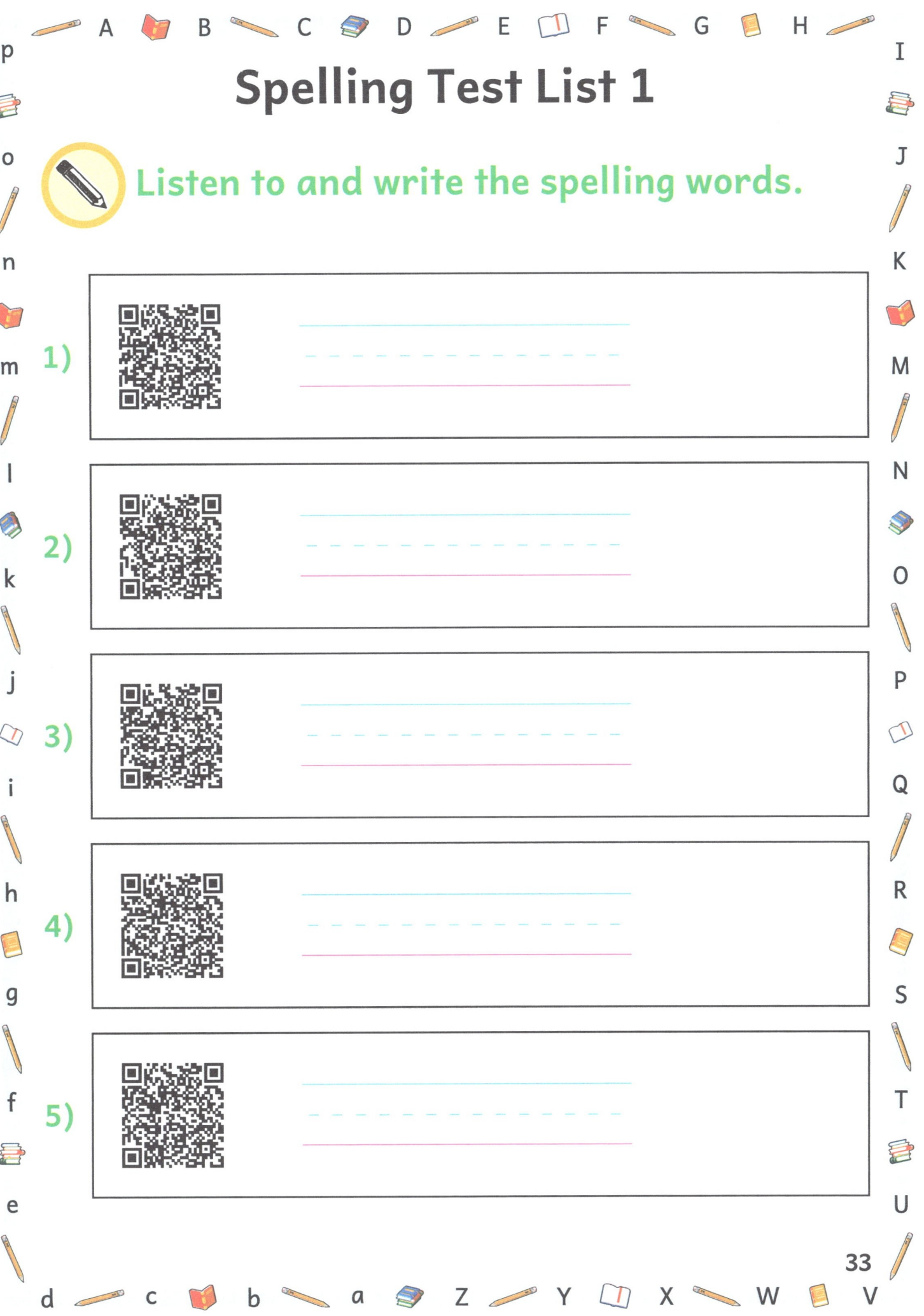

Listen to and write the spelling words.

1)

2)

3)

4)

5)

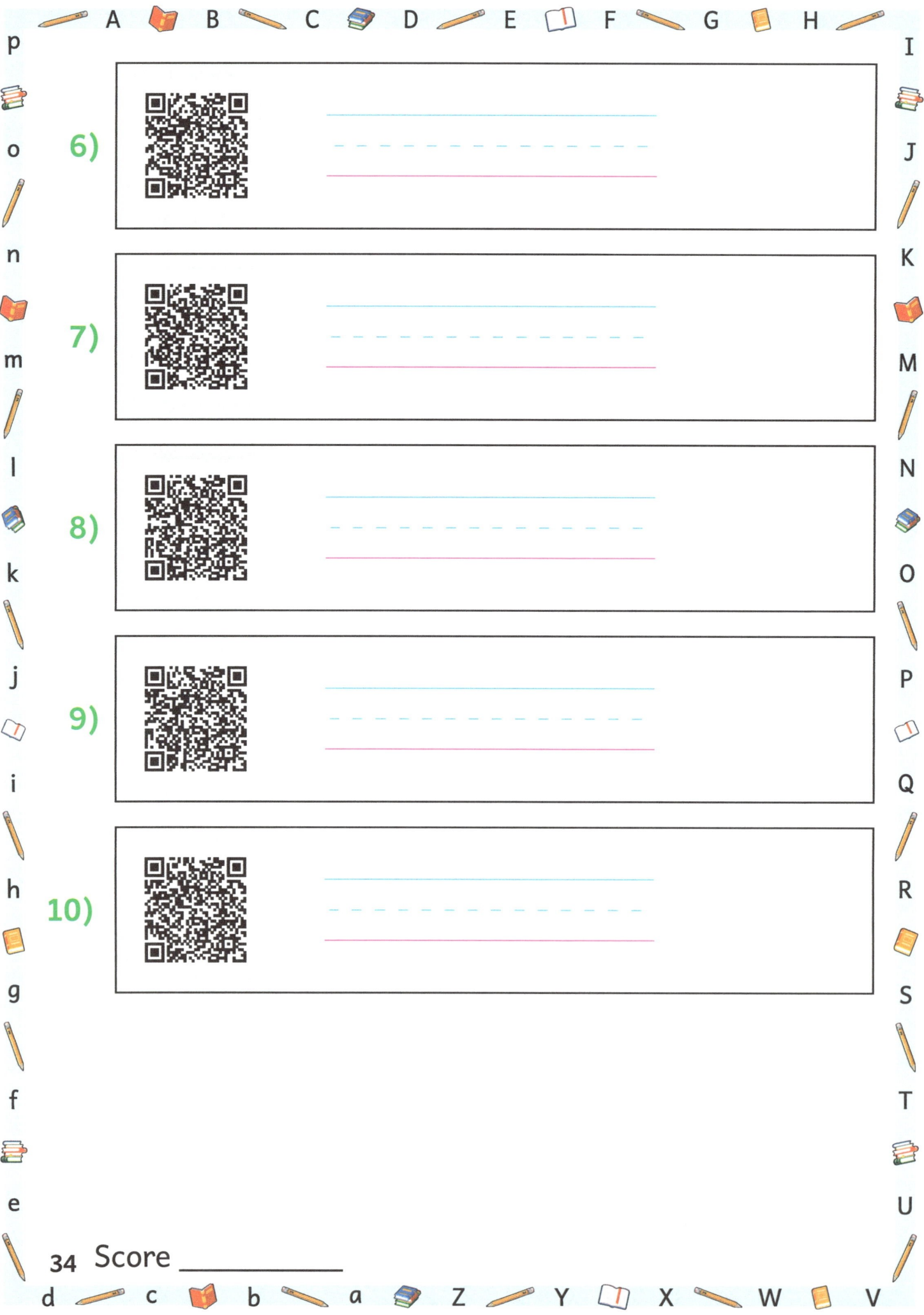

6)

7)

8)

9)

10)

Score _____

4. SPELLING LIST 2: Part 1

Learn:

- Divide and read two-syllable words.

- Spell and read words from List 2.

WRITING PHONOGRAM REVIEW

 **Listen to and write the phonograms.**
Underline any multi-letter phonograms.

WORKING WITH WORDS

The words in List 2 are closed syllables. The words end with two consonant letters. The words in this Lesson end with the consonant digraphs **th**, **sh**, or **ch**.

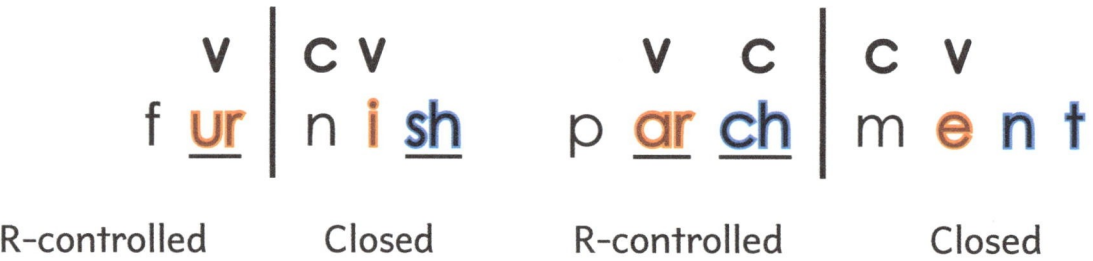

v | c v
f <u>ur</u> | n **i** <u>sh</u>

R-controlled   Closed

v | c | c v
p <u>ar</u> | <u>ch</u> | m **e** n t

R-controlled   Closed

 **Mark, divide, and read the VCCV and VCV words.**

Remember, underline the multi-letter phonograms first.

Jethro

skirmish

worship

poncho

chapter

urchin

zenith

shelter

Listen!

 **Circle the correct answers.**

1)	syllables	1	2	3	4

2)	sounds	1	2	3	4

 **Write and read.**

3) _____

 **Choose the correct answer.**

4) What is the syllable type?
   ○ vowel team
   ○ VCe
   ○ closed

Listen!

 **Circle the correct answers.**

5)	syllables	1	2	3	4

6)	sounds	1	2	3	4

 **Write and read.**

7) _____

 **Choose the correct answer.**

8) The vowel sound is ____.
   - ○ short
   - ○ long
   - ○ r-controlled

Listen!

? Circle the correct answers.

9) syllables   1   2   3   4

10) sounds   1   2   3   4

✏ Write and read.

11) _____

? Choose the correct answer.

12) Which reading rule does this word follow?
   ○ middle **s**
   ○ beginning **s**
   ○ 1st sound of **c**

Write the correct answers.
Complete the sentences.

| wish | with | such |

13) Tanner made a _____ after we sang to him.

14) We had _____ a great time at the party!

15) We ate cake _____ ice cream.

SCORE   CORRECT   RESCORE

Learn:

- Add missing consonant sounds.

- Spell and read words from List 2.

WRITING PHONOGRAM REVIEW

Listen to and write the phonograms.
Underline any multi-letter phonograms.

WORKING WITH WORDS

The words in this Lesson end with two consonant sounds. It is important to listen for both sounds.

 **Write the correct answers.**
Write the missing consonant in each word.

1)  mel__

2)  ha__d

3)  gol__

4) mi__k

5)  bu__p

6)  gif__

7)  a__t

8)  fis__

Listen!

Circle the correct answers.

9) syllables   1   2   3   4

10) sounds   1   2   3   4

Write and read.

11) _____

Choose the correct answer.

12) What is the syllable type?
    ○ r-controlled
    ○ closed
    ○ VCe

Listen!

 **Circle the correct answers.**

| 13) | syllables | 1 | 2 | 3 | 4 |

| 14) | sounds | 1 | 2 | 3 | 4 |

 **Write and read.**

15) _____

 **Choose the correct answer.**

16) Which reading rule does this word follow?
   - ○ beginning **s**
   - ○ double **s**
   - ○ middle **s**

Listen!

? **Circle the correct answers.**

17)
| syllables | 1 | 2 | 3 | 4 |

18)
| sounds | 1 | 2 | 3 | 4 |

✏ **Write and read.**

19) _____

? **Choose the correct answer.**

20) The vowel sound is ____.
- ○ long
- ○ short
- ○ r-controlled

 **Circle the correct answers.**

| 21) | syllables | 1 | 2 | 3 | 4 |

| 22) | sounds | 1 | 2 | 3 | 4 |

 **Write and read.**

23) _____

 **Choose the correct answer.**

24) Which reading rule does this word follow?
   ○ middle **s**
   ○ beginning **s**
   ○ double **s**

 **Write the correct answers.**
Sort the words in ABC order.

lift   just   fast

25) _____

26) _____

27) _____

 **Use the word in your own sentence.**

jump

28) _____

Learn:

- Use the floss rule to spell words.

- Spell and read words from List 2.

WRITING PHONOGRAM REVIEW

Listen to and write the phonograms.
Underline any multi-letter phonograms.

WORKING WITH WORDS

Spelling Rules

Floss Rule: Double **f**, **l**, **s**, and **z** at the end of a one-syllable word after one short vowel.

floss buzz

 **Write the correct answers.**
Add the ending letters to each word.

1)

she____

2)

gra____

3)

bu____

4)

gri____

5)

sni____

6)

che____

Listen!

 **Circle the correct answers.**

7) | syllables | 1 | 2 | 3 | 4 |

8) | sounds | 1 | 2 | 3 | 4 |

 **Write and read.**

9) _____

 **Choose the correct answer.**

10) What is the syllable type?

○ r-controlled

○ open

○ closed

Listen!

 **Circle the correct answers.**

| 11) | syllables | 1 | 2 | 3 | 4 |

| 12) | sounds | 1 | 2 | 3 | 4 |

 **Write and read.**

13) _____

 **Choose the correct answer.**

14) Which reading rule does this word follow?
- ○ double **s**
- ○ vowel teams
- ○ beginning **y**

Listen!

 **Circle the correct answers.**

15)	syllables	1	2	3	4

16)	sounds	1	2	3	4

 **Write and read.**

17) _____

 **Choose the correct answer.**

18) The vowel makes its ____ sound.
- ○ first
- ○ second
- ○ third

Circle the correct answers.
Which picture describes the sentence?

19) I turned **off** the light when I left.

20) Jessie had to stay home and **miss** the game.

21) We need to **pull** the weeds in our yard.

SCORE   CORRECT   RESCORE

PHONOGRAM REVIEW

 Listen to and circle the correct phonograms.

1)  a   o   oo

2)  t   h   d

3)  sh   ti   ci

4)  oe   oo   oa

5)  h   b   ch

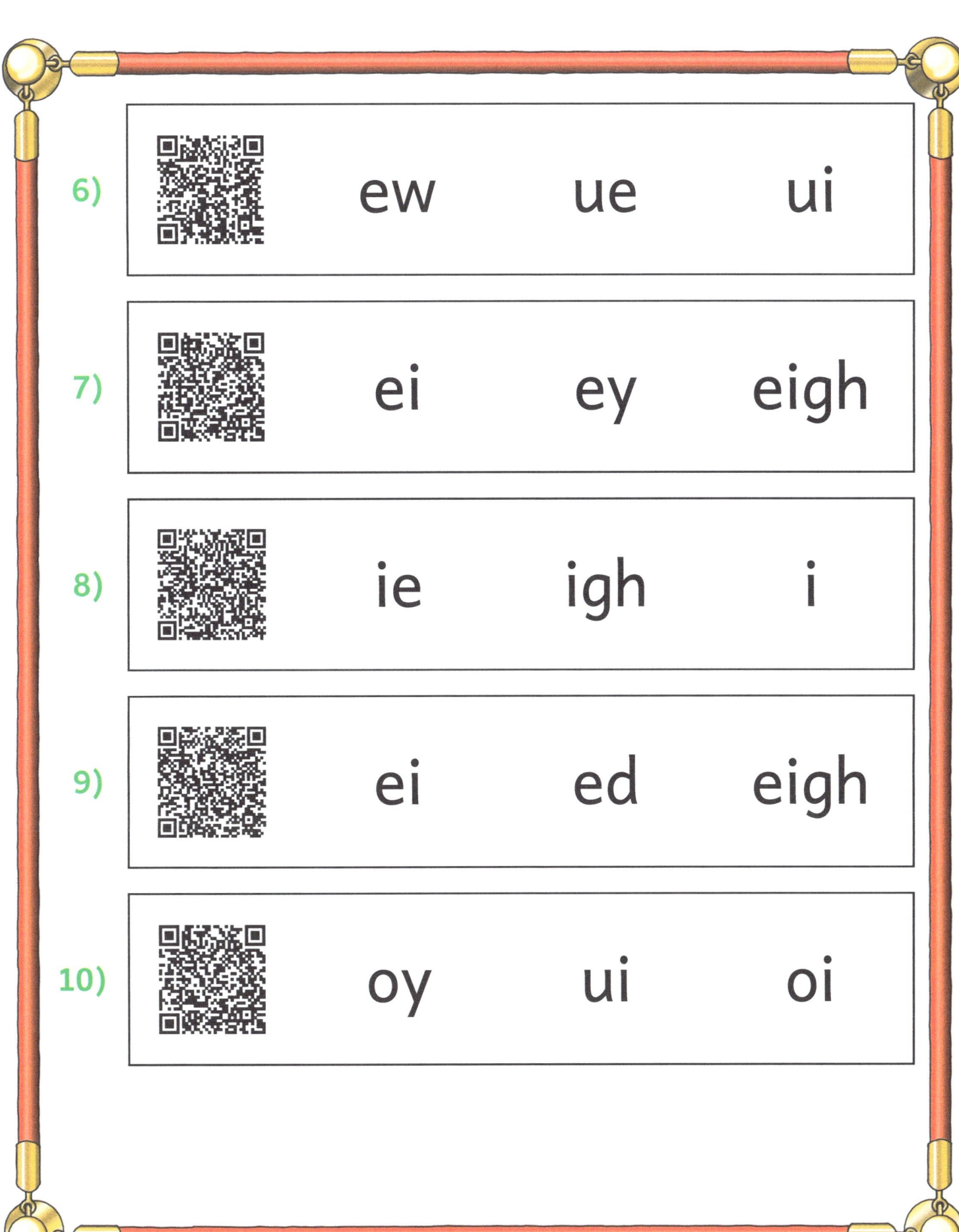

6)   ew   ue   ui

7)   ei   ey   eigh

8)   ie   igh   i

9)   ei   ed   eigh

10)   oy   ui   oi

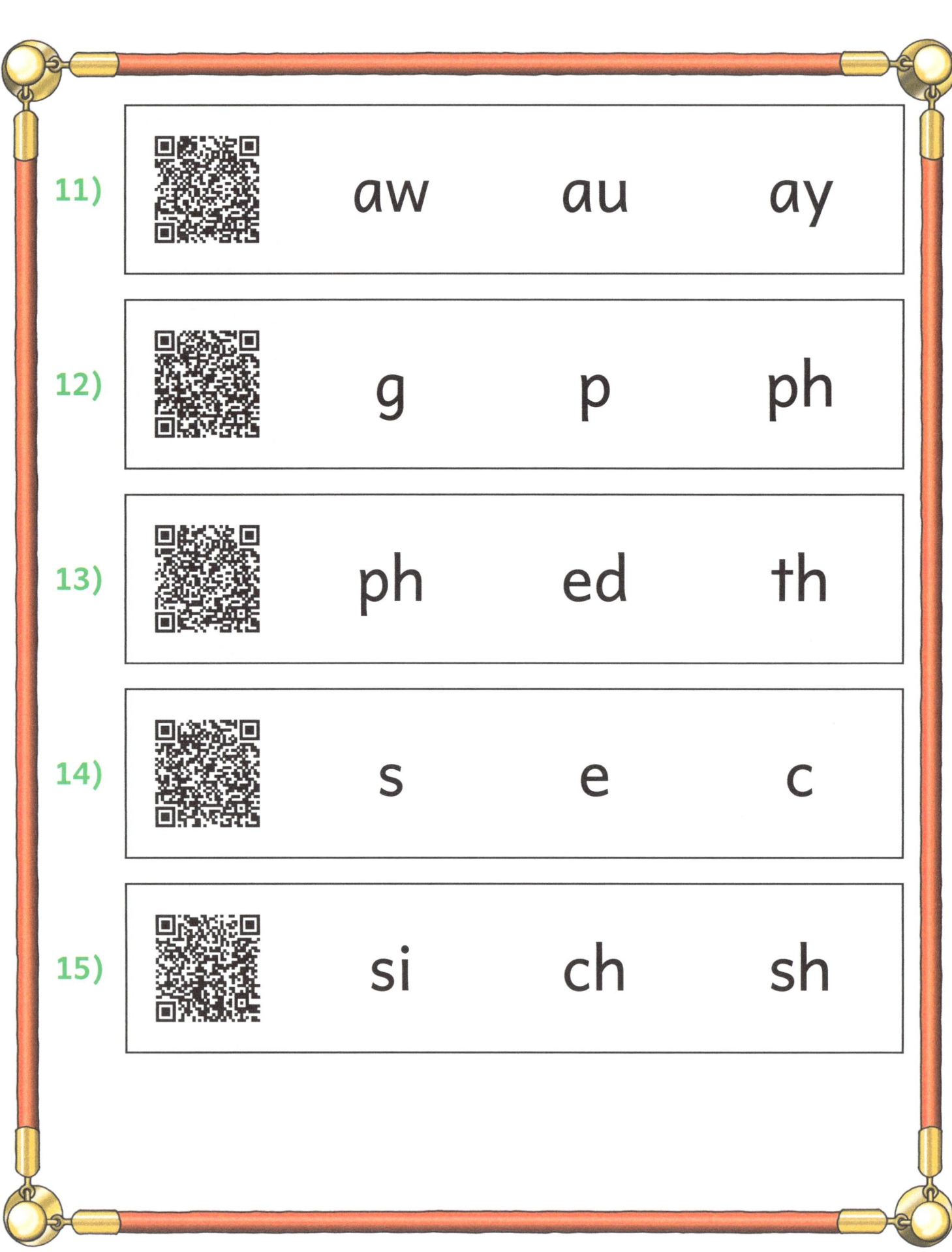

11) aw   au   ay

12) g   p   ph

13) ph   ed   th

14) s   e   c

15) si   ch   sh

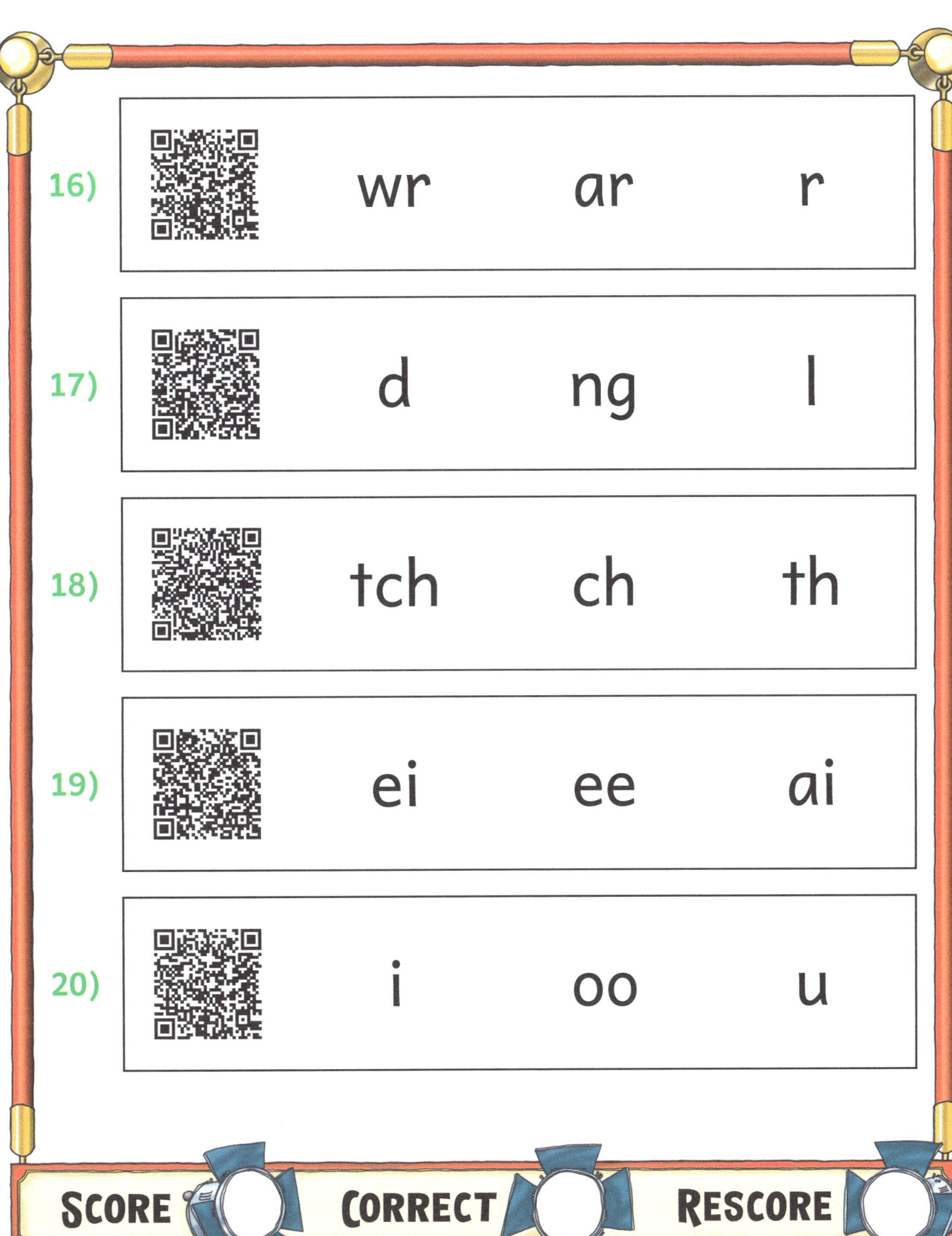

16) wr   ar   r

17) d   ng   l

18) tch   ch   th

19) ei   ee   ai

20) i   oo   u

SCORE   CORRECT   RESCORE

SPELLING LIST 2 REVIEW

 **Write the correct answers.**
Write the words in the boxes.

wish   jump   such

1)   2)   3)

pull   fast   with

4)   5)   6)

just   miss   lift   off

7)   8)   9)

10)

58

READER 9: "Bix the Mighty Hero"

Reader 9 has the tricky word *was*. When the letter **a** is in a short word or syllable, we often shorten it to the short **u**.

Tricky Word
w**a**s

 **Listen to the sound of a in this sentence.**

The sof**a** w**a**s dirty, so they took it **a**way **a** long time **a**go.

 **Write the correct answers.**
Complete the sentences.

away   was   what

1) I liked _____ you gave me for a gift.

2) The bird flew _____ when I got close to it.

3) It _____ too dark to play at the park.

59

Reader 9

Bix the Mighty Hero

? Choose the correct answers.

4) What did Bix want to be?

○ a dolphin

○ a hero

○ a sea king

5) What did Pip do as the sea king?

○ He threw the palm trees off the beach.

○ He spent money on a big crown.

○ He invited the pals to a party.

6) Why did Pip wake up?

○ A palm tree fell down.

○ It started to rain on the beach.

○ Bix yelled in his sleep.

Phonogram Test 14

Listen to and write the correct phonograms.
Underline any multi-letter phonograms.

1)

2)

3)

4)

5)

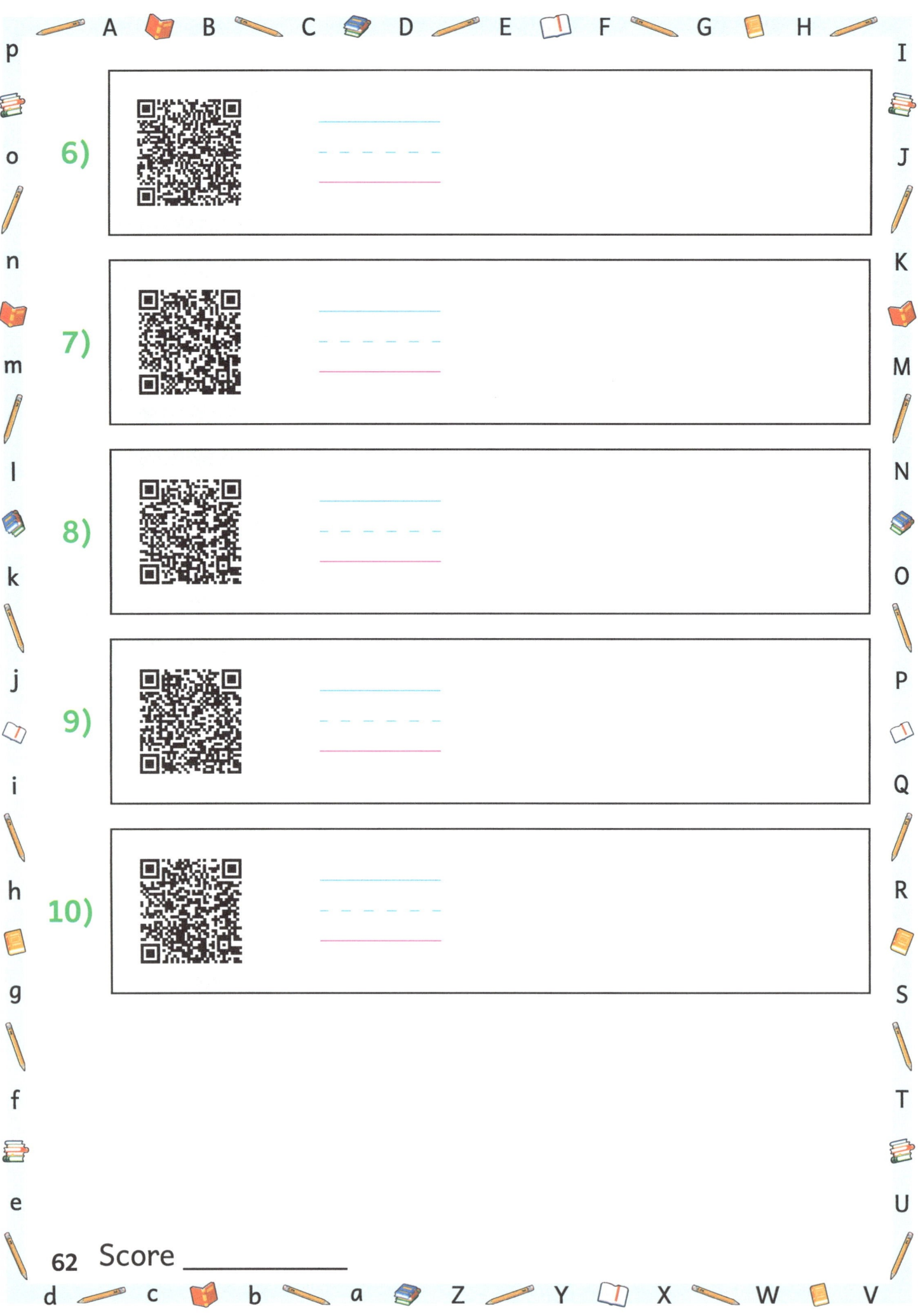

Score _____

Spelling Test List 2

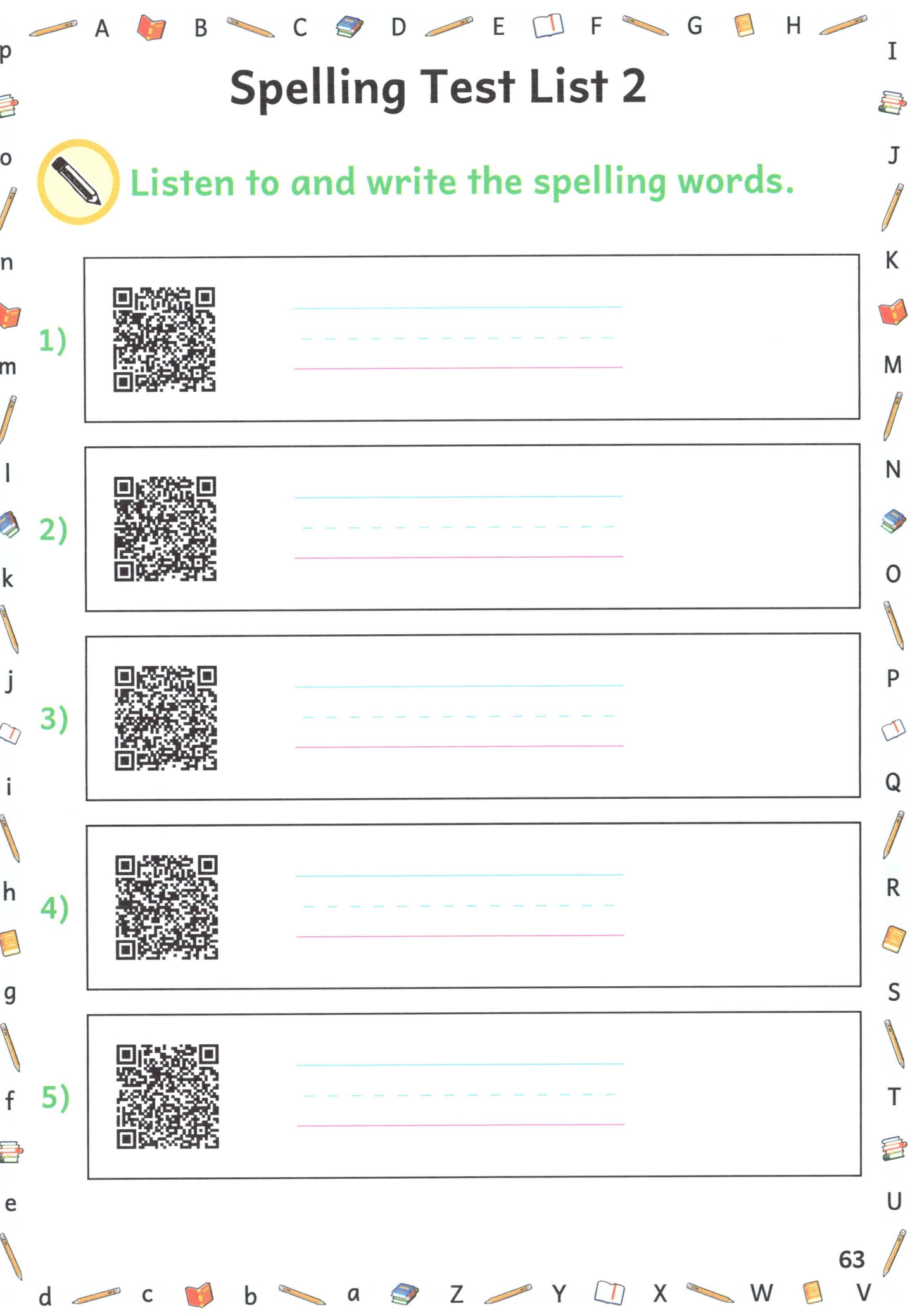

Listen to and write the spelling words.

1)

2)

3)

4)

5)

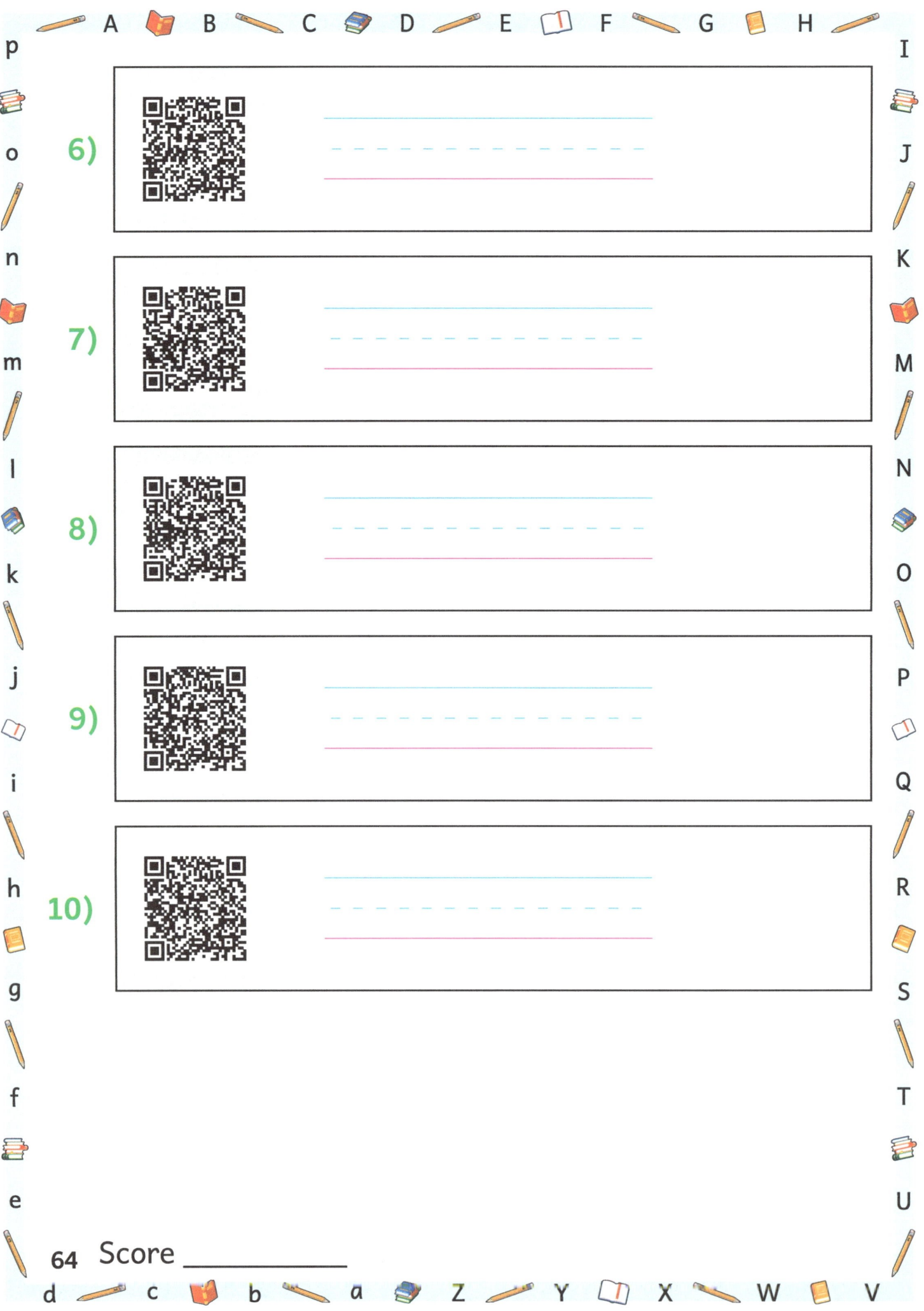

Score _____

Learn:

- Use the ending **ck** rule to spell words.

- Spell and read words from List 3.

WRITING PHONOGRAM REVIEW

 **Listen to and write the phonograms.**
Underline any multi-letter phonograms.

WORKING WITH WORDS

Spelling Rules

Ending **ck**: Use **ck** to spell the **k** sound at the end of a one-syllable base word after one short vowel.

d**uck** qu**ack**

✏️ **Write the correct answers.**
Add the ending letters to each word.

1)

blo____

2)

tru____

3)

sti____

4)

cli____

5)

sli____

6)

chi____

Listen!

? **Circle the correct answers.**

7) | syllables | 1 2 3 4 |

8) | sounds | 1 2 3 4 |

 **Write and read.**

9) _____

? **Choose the correct answer.**

10) What is the syllable type?
   ○ closed
   ○ open
   ○ VCe

Listen!

? **Circle the correct answers.**

11) | syllables | 1   2   3   4 |

12) | sounds | 1   2   3   4 |

 **Write and read.**

13) _____

 **Choose the correct answer.**

14) Which reading rule does this word follow?
   ○ 2nd sound of **c**
   ○ beginning **s**
   ○ r-controlled vowels

Listen!

 **Circle the correct answers.**

15) | syllables | 1 2 3 4

16) | sounds | 1 2 3 4

 **Write and read.**

17) _____

 **Choose the correct answer.**

18) The vowel sound is ____.
- ○ short
- ○ long
- ○ r-controlled

Write the correct answers.
Complete the sentences.

| black | snack | rock |

19) Let's stop to eat a _____.

20) Rick set down the _____ bag.

21) I will sit on this big _____.

SCORE ⟲   CORRECT ⟲   RESCORE ⟲

ACTIVITY: ck or k?

Use digraph **ck** after a short vowel sound. Use the letter **k** after any other vowel sound or a consonant.

crack   **shark**   **chalk**   **beak**

Write ck or k to complete each word.

boo____   ki____   sta____

par____   sha____   chee____

Learn:

- Divide and read compound words.
- Spell and read words from List 3.

Vocabulary:

compound word *[kŏm´pownd werd]* – a word made from two base words

---

WRITING PHONOGRAM REVIEW

Listen to and write the phonograms.
Underline any multi-letter phonograms.

WORKING WITH WORDS

A **compound word** is made of two base words. Together, the words create a new word.

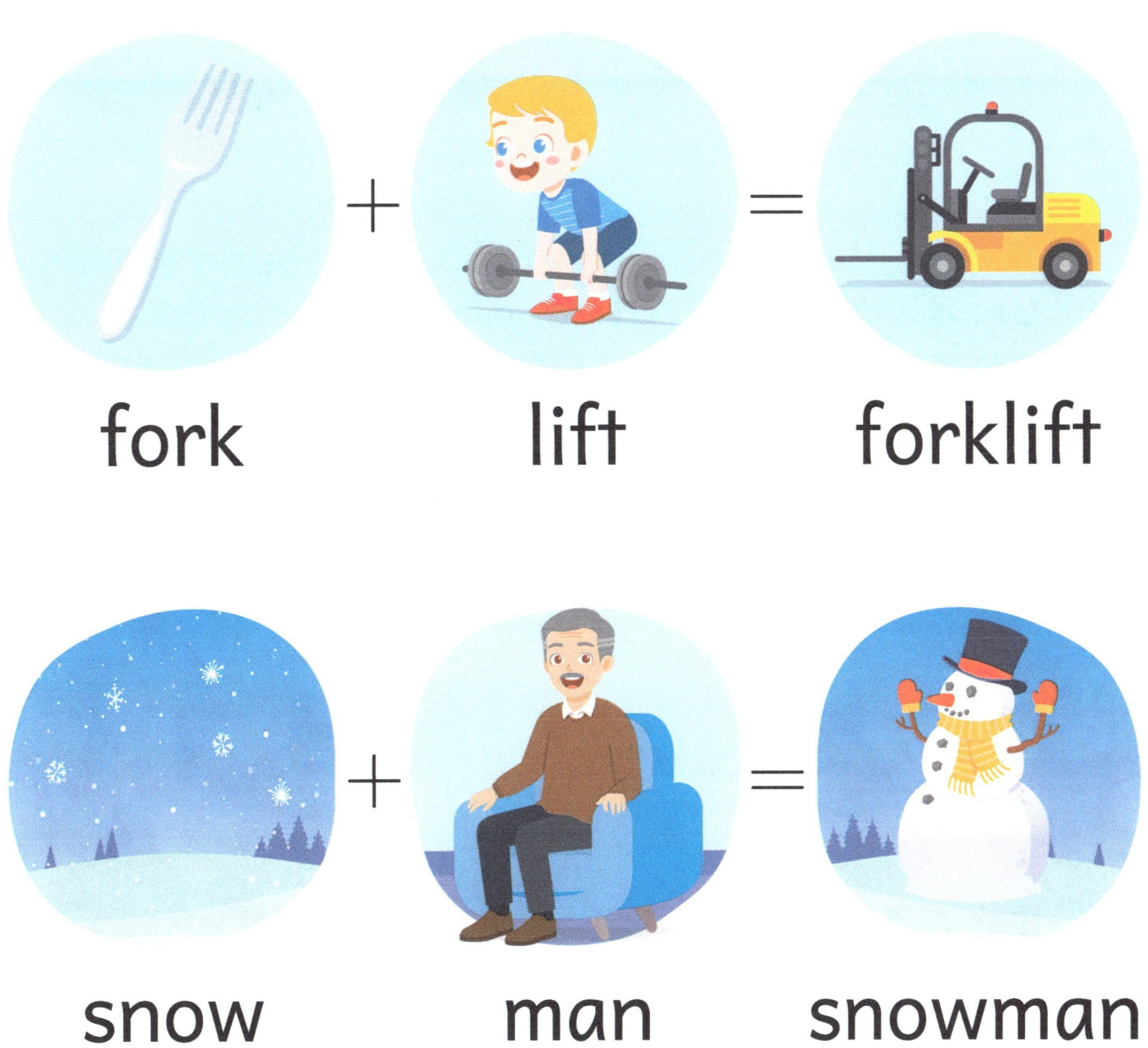

fork   +   lift   =   forklift

snow   +   man   =   snowman

We divide compound words between the two base words. That can be tricky if you need to sound out the word. Sometimes, you can use the VCCV or VCV patterns.

Word 1   Word 2   Word 1   Word 2

Mark, divide, and read the compound words.
Use the VCCV and VCV patterns or look for the two words. Remember, underline the multi-letter phonograms first.

airlift

bedrock

daybed

seashell

teacup

peanut

flatbed

carhop

blackbird

starfish

Listen!

 **Circle the correct answers.**

1)	syllables	1	2	3	4

2)	sounds	1	2	3	4

 **Write and read.**

3) _____

 **Choose the correct answer.**

4) Which reading rule does this word follow?
   - ○ 1st sound of **c**
   - ○ 2nd sound of **c**
   - ○ **g** before **e**, **i**, or **y**

Listen!

 **Circle the correct answers.**

5) | syllables | 1 | 2 | 3 | 4 |

6) | sounds | 1 | 2 | 3 | 4 |

 **Write and read.**

7) _____

 **Choose the correct answer.**

8) Which reading rule does this word follow?
   - ○ beginning **y**
   - ○ 1st sound of **c**
   - ○ **o** before **m**, **n**, or **v**

Listen!

 **Circle the correct answers.**

9) | syllables | 1 2 3 4

10) | sounds | 1 2 3 4

 **Write and read.**

11) _____

 **Choose the correct answer.**

12) What is the syllable type?
- ○ closed
- ○ vowel team
- ○ VCe

Listen!

 **Circle the correct answers.**

| 13) | syllables | 1 | 2 | 3 | 4 |

| 14) | sounds | 1 | 2 | 3 | 4 |

 **Write and read.**

15) _____

 **Choose the correct answer.**

16) The vowel sound is ____.
    ○ r-controlled
    ○ long
    ○ short

 **Write the correct answers.**
Write the words in ABC order.

clock   brick   trick

17) _____

18) _____

19) _____

 **Use the word in your own sentence.**

cluck

20) _____

SCORE   CORRECT   RESCORE

9. SPELLING LIST 3: Part 3

Learn:

- Divide and read compound words.

- Spell and read words from List 3.

WRITING PHONOGRAM REVIEW

Listen to and write the phonograms.
Underline any multi-letter phonograms.

WORKING WITH WORDS

These compound words cannot be divided with the VCCV or VCV patterns. You will have to divide between the two words. Look for one of your spelling words from this Unit to help you.

take|off
word 1 word 2

✏️ **Divide and read the compound words.**
Remember, underline the multi-letter phonograms first.

kickoff   fastball

jumpsuit   milkman

offhand   within

caveman   clockwork

Listen!

 **Circle the correct answers.**

1)	syllables	1	2	3	4

2)	sounds	1	2	3	4

 **Write and read.**

3) _____

 **Choose the correct answer.**

4) Which reading rule does this word follow?
   - ○ double **s**
   - ○ 3rd sound of **a**
   - ○ beginning **s**

Listen!

 **Circle the correct answers.**

5)	syllables	1	2	3	4

6)	sounds	1	2	3	4

 **Write and read.**

7) _____

 **Choose the correct answer.**

8) What is the syllable type?
   - ○ closed
   - ○ open
   - ○ r-controlled

Listen!

Circle the correct answers.

9) syllables   1   2   3   4

10) sounds   1   2   3   4

 **Write and read.**

11) _____

Choose the correct answer.

12) The vowel sound is ____.
- ○ r-controlled
- ○ long
- ○ short

Circle the correct answers.
Which picture describes the sentence?

13) We saw a car **wreck** on the road.

14) It is good to stay home when you are **sick**.

15) Chuck put the name tag around his **neck**.

SCORE   CORRECT   RESCORE

PHONOGRAM REVIEW

Listen to and circle the correct phonograms.

1)  ea   ei   ey

2)  r   n   m

3)  th   t   ti

4)  ow   r   wr

5)  ear   ar   wor

6) o a u

7) ow au qu

8) v f ph

9) igh oi i

10) ui ue oi

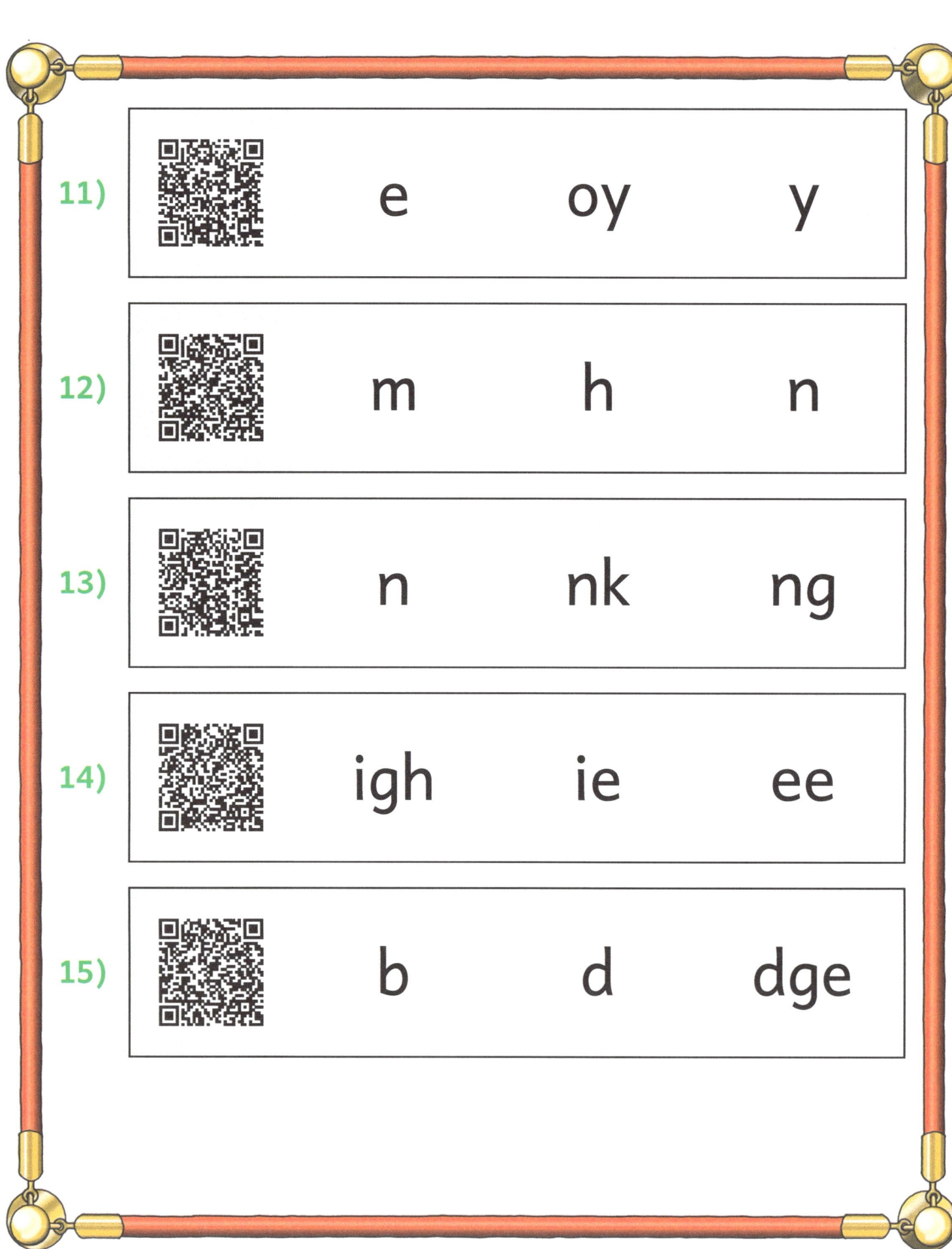

11) e   oy   y

12) m   h   n

13) n   nk   ng

14) igh   ie   ee

15) b   d   dge

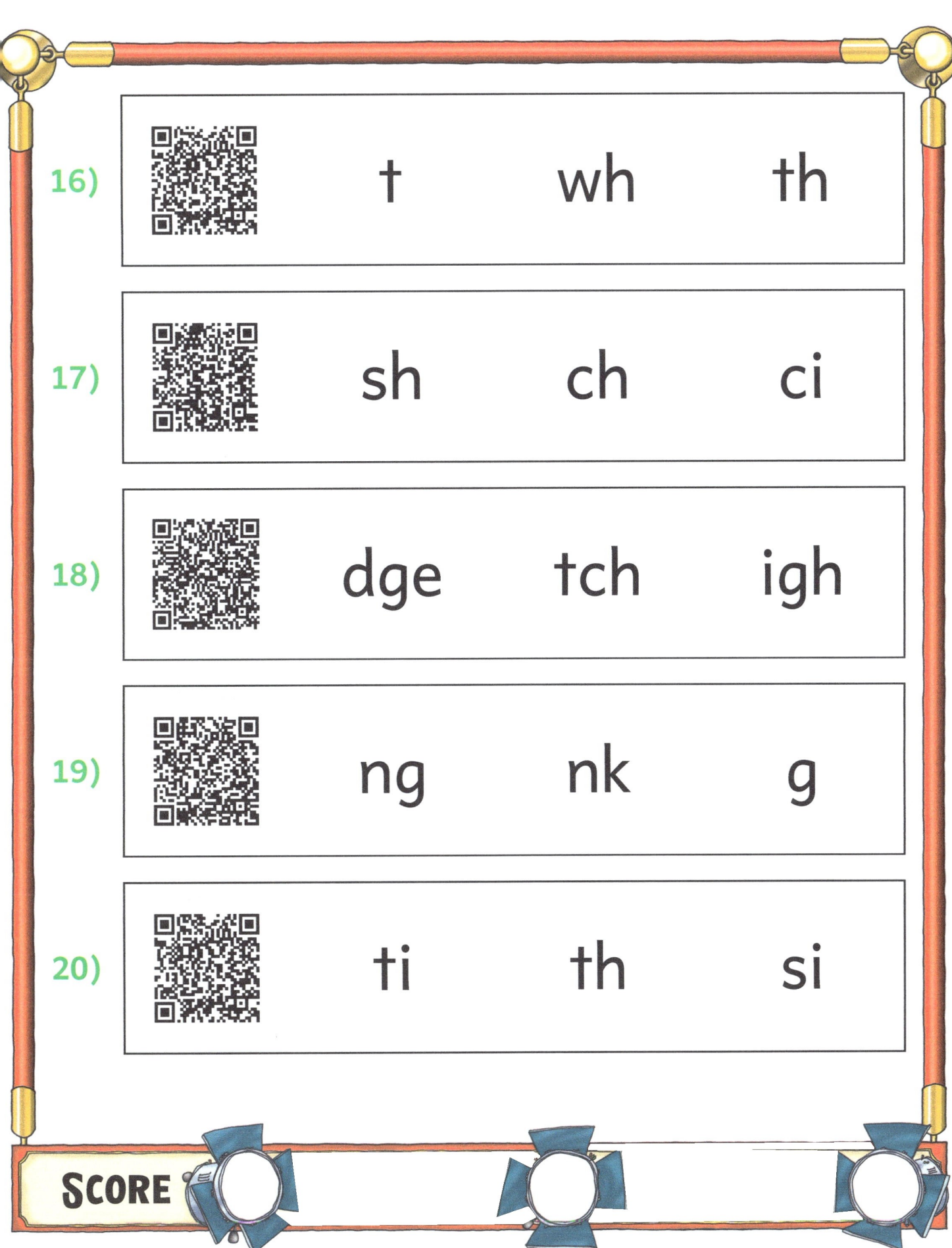

16)   t   wh   th

17)   sh   ch   ci

18)   dge   tch   igh

19)   ng   nk   g

20)   ti   th   si

SCORE

SPELLING LIST 3 REVIEW

? **Listen to and circle the correct words.**

1)  brick   snack   black

2)  black   clock   cluck

3)  rock   wreck   clock

4)  rock   brick   wreck

5)  trick   sick   brick

6) snack   trick   sick

7) neck   snack   sick

8) snack   neck   wreck

9) clock   trick   cluck

10) wreck   rock   brick

Reader 10 has the tricky word *does*. The vowel team **oe** makes the short **u** sound. This only happens in the words *does* and *doesn't*.

Tricky Word
do e s

Listen to the forms of does in this sentence.

Jenny **doesn't** know if she will **do** what she **did** last time.

Write the correct answers.
Complete the sentences.

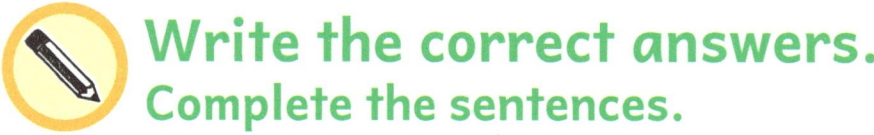

do   did   does

1) Grace _____ a great job last night.

2) Paul will _____ all of the dishes.

3) Blake still _____ not know how to cook.

 **Choose the correct answers.**

4) What sound did the chicken make?

○ tweet, tweet

○ chirp, chirp

○ cluck, cluck

5) What was in the bucket?

○ a brick

○ a trick snake

○ a chicken

6) Why was the chicken happy?

○ It was no longer stuck.

○ It found a toy car.

○ It made new pals.

Phonogram Test 15

Listen to and write the correct phonograms.
Underline any multi-letter phonograms.

1)

2)

3)

4)

5)

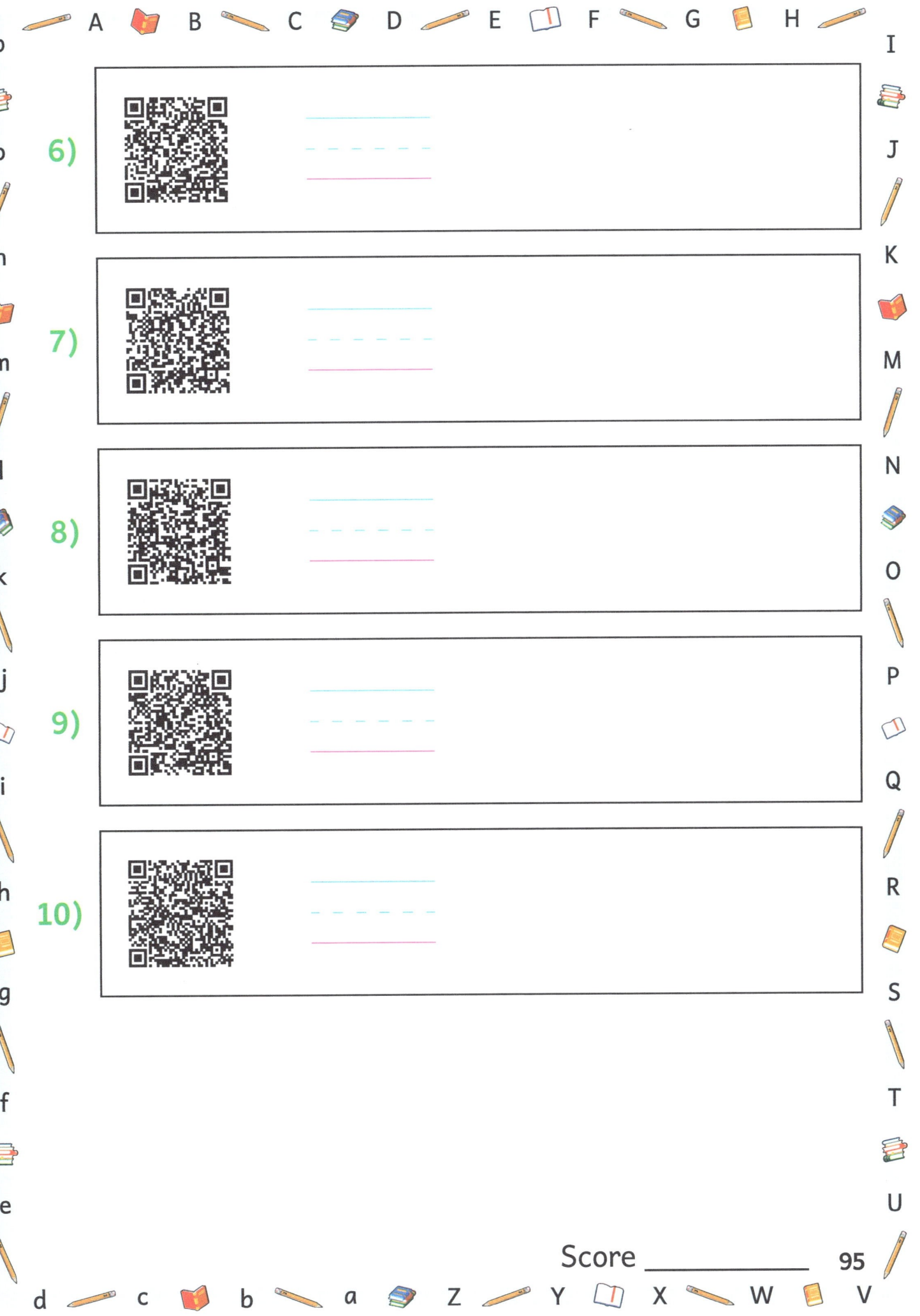

A   B   C   D   E   F   G   H   I
J   K   M   N   O   P   Q   R   S   T   U   V   W   X   Y   Z
a   b   c   d   e   f   g   h   i   j   k   l   m   n   o   p

6)

7)

8)

9)

10)

Score _____ 95

Spelling Test List 3

Listen to and write the spelling words.

1)

2)

3)

4)

5)

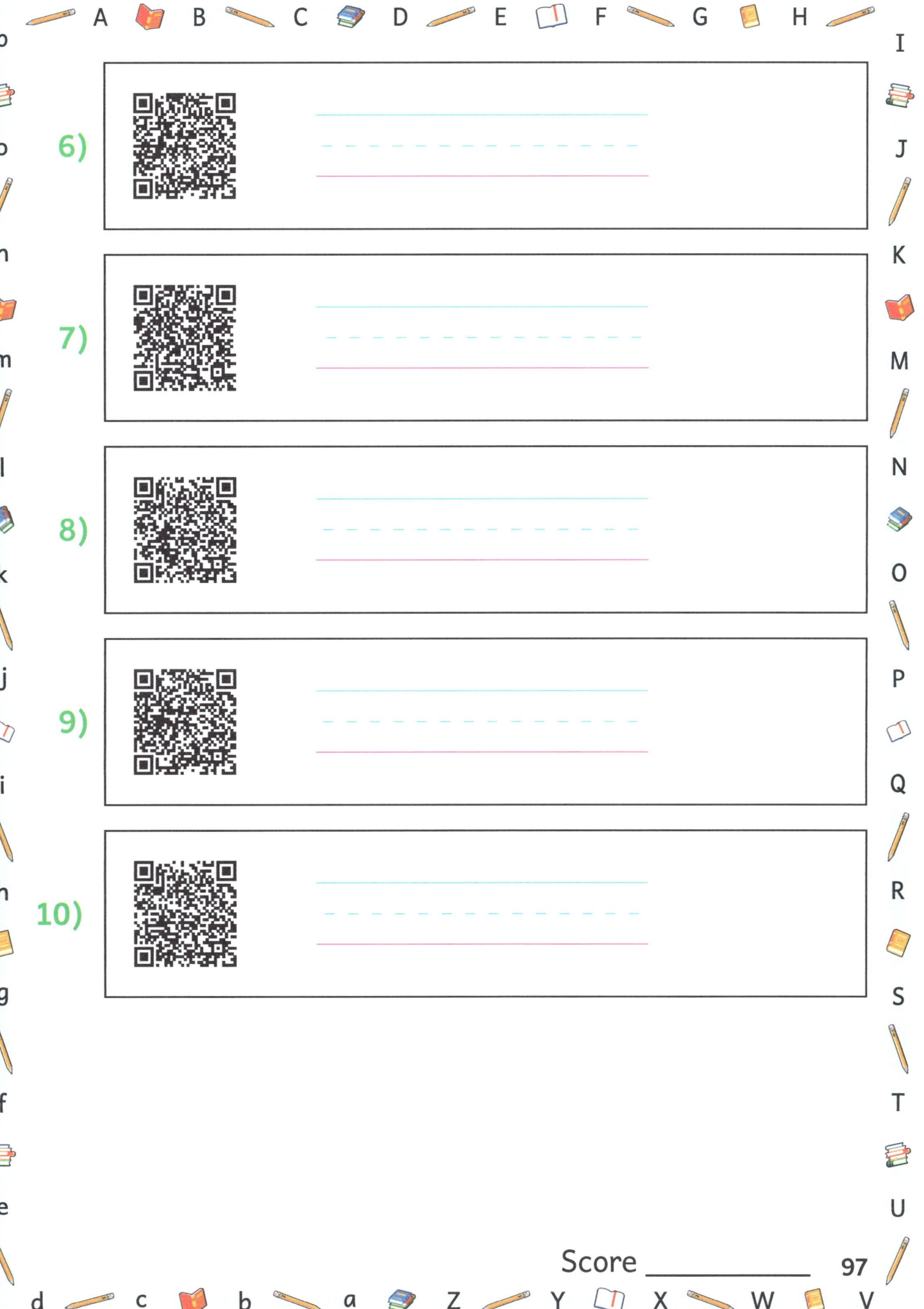

To Do:
For best results, fold then unfold lines before building.

 **Head**

- Fold into a box shape.

- Secure tabs with glue.

 **Body**

- Fold into a box shape.

- Secure tabs with glue.

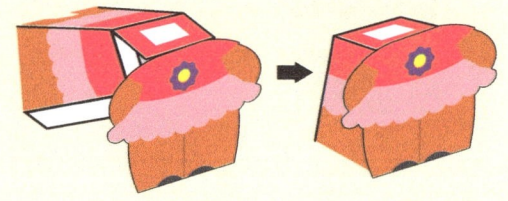

 **Build**

- Attach head to body with glue.